101 Yo-Yo Tricks

The Ultimate Collection of the Coolest Yo-Yo Tricks

is without contract or any type of guarantee assurance.

The trademarks that are used are without any consent, and the publication of the trademark is without permission or backing by the trademark owner. All trademarks and brands within this book are for clarifying purposes only and are the owned by the owners themselves, not affiliated with this document.

Introduction

While a man named Donald Duncan is generally credited for the first yo-yo fad of the United States, he was far from being the inventor of the yo-yo. In fact, the popular toy is considered the second oldest in the world, right behind the baby doll. Some of its earliest known usage is in ancient Greece, where the toy was made of terracotta, metal or wood. It gained popularity in Europe and the Orient.

The yo-yo was also known in the Philippines—but for a different reason. In the Philippines, the yo-yo had studs and sharp edges attached to it and it was attached to a thick rope that was several meters long. Then, it was flung to kill prey or injure enemies during war.

Since the 1920s, the yo-yo has been in production in the United States. It is a great hobby toy for young and old. For those who are tired of the same old 'up and down' of tossing the yo-yo, learning tricks can make yo-yoing fun and challenging.

As you read this book, you will learn tricks with various levels of difficulty. We will start with basic tricks and picture tricks (when you hold the yo-yo still and make a picture) and then move to more advanced techniques. By the end of this book, not only will you be able to do all sorts of challenging and fun moves with the yo-yo, you will have become a master at a great hobby.

All you need to get started is a responsive yo-yo with a sleeper position. A sleeper yo-yo is simply one that uses a loop around the center of the yo-yo, rather than a fixed point. This increases responsiveness and lets the string move freely within the yo-yo. Now, it is time to grab your yo-yo and start practicing!

Chapter One: Yo-yo Tricks- The Basics

When you are ready to get started, knowing these tricks will give you practice and lay the foundation for more advanced yo-yoing skills in the future.

The Basic Gravity Pull

This is the basic up and down motion that you should master before beginning any tricks. Start with the end of the yo-yo looped around your middle finger and the palm of your hand facing the ground. Allow the yo-yo to fall toward the ground and when it reaches the end of its string, jerk your hand so the yo-yo jumps back up into your hand.

The Throw Down

This is a simple technique, but there are many variations of it that are used in more advanced tricks, so it is good to practice. Start with your palm facing upward and stand the yo-yo up on end, so it is positioned between your middle finger and your thumb. Then, flick your wrist to throw your yo-yo straight toward the ground, using an overhand motion. Tug on it slightly when you are ready for it to return to your hand.

The Sleeper

This yo-yoing position is used in close to 90% of yo-yo moves, so it is something important to master. Hold your hand out in front of you so that the palm is facing upward and then throw the yo-yo as if you were whipping a fastball toward the ground. The yo-yo should remain in place, spinning, while you turn your palm over. If the tension in the string is at the right level, the yo-yo will continue spinning at the end of the string until you jerk it upward and back into your hand.

Reverse Sleeper

The difference between this trick and the previous one is the way the yo-yo spins. Start as if you were throwing a Sleeper, positioning the yo-yo so it is aligned with your shoulder. This time, however, use an overhand instead of an underhand motion so the yo-yo spins the opposite way. It is important that the yo-yo is thrown straight down, otherwise it may go sideways. As usual, you will use a quick jerk so the yo-yo comes back home.

Elevator

To do this trick, start by throwing a Sleeper yo-yo. While it is spinning, use your yo-yo hand to form a letter 'C'. Use your free hand to grab the string with your pointer finger and pull it through the 'C' shape that you formed. This should bring the yo-yo close to your hand. When you are ready to end the trick once the yo-yo is close, drop it so it quickly falls to the ground. Then, jerk upward so the yo-yo comes back home.

Walk the Dog

If you know anyone with a yo-yoing hobby (even a kid), you have probably heard of the popular trick Walk the Dog. Walk the Dog is a variation of the Sleeper—just throw the Sleeper forward and then swing forward, setting the yo-yo on the ground. Allow the natural spinning motion to guide the yo-yo along the ground and give it a tug when you are ready for the yo-yo to return to your hand.

Walk the Cat

The joke of this trick is that you can never get cats to do what you want them to do. Start with a Reverse Sleeper, allowing the yo-yo to come to a rest on the ground as you slowly walk forward. The yo-yo should be walking opposite you, behind you. The joke is when you act like the 'cat' has jerked you back because you were not expecting it to move in that direction. Use a quick flick of the wrist to bring the yo-yo back to your hand.

Through the Hoop

To do this trick, which is similar to "Walk the Dog," you are going to toss a hard Sleeper. Let the yo-yo swing behind your leg and then set it on the ground. Walk the Dog between both your legs. When you have finished the trick, tug the string back so that the 'dog' goes back between your legs and then around them, leaving it in front of you so you can jerk it back into your hand.

Rock the Baby

Begin with a Sleeper throw, before raising the yo-yo up so that the top of the string is just above your head. Then, take your free hand and place it between your body and the yo-yo string, with the palm toward you and the fingers outstretched. Use the tip of your thumb and your pinky to catch the string about one-third of the way down the string.

Next, use your yo-yo hand to grab the string 4 to 5 inches above the yo-yo. As you bring up your yo-yoing hand so it is above the free hand, you will form a triangle shape. This is the cradle. The yo-yo should dangle in the 'cradle' and now you can 'rock the baby' by moving the yo-yo forward and back.

Eating Pizza

This fun trick makes it look as if you are eating a slice of pizza. Start by pinching the string about one-third of the way down with your free hand. Then, pinch the string closer to the yo-yo using your yo-yo hand. Take your thumb and forefinger on your free hand to spread open the top of the pizza, creating the triangular shape. Make some sound effects as you take a 'bite' of the end of the pizza. As you do this, let go of the string you pinched with your yo-yo hand, to let the pizza shrink in size as you are eating.

The Forward Pass

If you have learned the Throw Down, you are ready to practice this trick. Position the yo-yo in your hand like you would if performing Throw Down. Instead of holding your arm out in front of you, however, drop it to the side of your body. The back of your hand should be forward facing. Swing your arm forward while flicking your wrist, throwing the yo-yo forward. At the end of the length of string, turn your hand so your palm is facing upward and try to catch it. You may not be able to the first few times—but work on the trajectory of making the yo-yo hit your hand when it comes back.

Skin the Cat

Throw a hard Sleeper in front of you before using your index finger on your free hand to slide up the string in front of the finger the yo-yo is on. Then, use the same hand and move it slightly upward while you use the hand holding the yo-yo to pull backward. As the yo-yo returns to your hand, flip it upward with the free hand and jerk backward with the yo-yo hand when it is about six inches away. Instead of catching the yo-yo, use a Forward pass to finish the trick.

Around the World

Keeping the right amount of slack in your yo-yo string is essential for this trick. Begin with a Forward Pass, but instead of bringing the yo-yo back home when it reaches the end of the string, allow it to remain in Sleeper position while you swing it full circle. Bring it over the shoulder of the hand you are holding the yo-yo in and swing it behind your back. When it returns to the starting point, use a jerking motion so the yo-yo returns to your hand. You should always use caution when performing this trick, so you do not injure yourself or anyone (or anything) around you.

Under Mount

The Over Mount and the Under Mount are the two most basic mounts and by mastering them, you will be ready to tackle more difficult yo-yo mounting tricks. For the Under Mount, start by throwing a Sleeper. Allow the yo-yo to swing toward you and put out the pointer finger of your free hand to catch the string about two-thirds of the way down. Let the yo-yo continue its trajectory, coming up and around to catch the yo-yo string.

Once on the string, bring your hands closer to each other to create a little slack. Then, pull your free hand toward your body, creating a 'J' shape with the yo-yo hanging at the bend in the bottom of the 'J'. As you improve your skills, you will find yourself ready to try a Ferris Wheel Dismount, which is a great way to transition out of the Under Mount. You could also do a simple mount by tightening the string by separating your hands, so the yo-yo follows its trajectory back around. When it gets to the end of its string, jerk on it to bring it back home.

Over Mount
The Over Mount is very similar to the last trick, except the yo-yo swings away from your body to mount the yo-yo. Start by throwing a Sleeper, but use the index finger of your free hand to pull back on the string. This should make the yo-yo jump up. Create slack as before once the yo-yo has mounted the string to form a backward 'J' shape. To get out of this, catapult the yo-yo as you would when doing an Under Mount so it goes around before coming back to your hand. You can also dismount using a simple "Front-style Bind," which will be discussed later.

Over and Under Mount

To do this trick, you will begin with an Under Mount. Once the yo-yo is mounted on the string, pull the string taut so the yo-yo dismounts and starts to move around. Then, stick out your middle finger of your free hand so that it wraps around that and continues forward, mounting on the opposite side of the string. Tighten the string so the yo-yo jumps out of the Over Mount and then go back into the Under Mount, switching between the two until you are satisfied. When you are finished, use the dismount of your choice to finish the trick and bring the yo-yo back to your hand.

The Breakaway

Bend your arm as if you were making a muscle, with your yo-yo in the hand of the arm you are using. Then, swing your arm in front of your body and let go of the yo-yo, while bringing your elbow down hard. The yo-yo should fly out across your body and then swing down. When the yo-yo is down, use your yo-yoing arm to swing across the front of your body, making an arc toward the side opposite your yo-yo arm. Give the yo-yo a second to hand at the end of the string and as the spin slows, jerk the string to bring it back to your hand.

The Pinwheel

For this trick, which is artful and easy, start by throwing a hard Sleeper. Then, use your free hand to pinch the string, between your index finger and thumb, about two-thirds of the way down. Move your yo-yo hand down as you move the free hand away from your body, up and to the side. Then, use the hand to swing the yo-yo in Pinwheel-like circles, three or more times. When you are ready for the final turn, throw the yo-yo forward and up. Once you release the string, jerk it back and catch it with your yo-yo hand.

Butterfly

Also called the four-leaf clover, this picture trick is fairly easy to learn. Start by throwing a Sleeper. Then, drape the string over the index and middle finger on your free hand. Weave this through to hang over your ring finger and pinky finger on your yo-yo hand. Then, use the last two fingers on your free hand to weave the yo-yo string through again. Next, you will take the index and middle fingers on your yo-yo hand and grab the extra length of string, pulling it upward. Then, flip the yo-yo up and around the front so that it loops around all the segments of string near the middle. Separate your fingers apart to complete the picture.

Flying Saucer

To do this trick, start by throwing the yo-yo downward, but slightly to the side opposite the hand you are holding the yo-yo in (i.e., if you are right handed you will throw toward the left). As the yo-yo reaches the end of the string, use your free hand to pinch the string and pull it upward, to about waist height. The yo-yo should start to spin, tilted to the side. As the yo-yo turns on its side, use the finger of your free hand to guide it, so that it moves in a circle. When you are ready to bring it back home, release the string and let the yo-yo move back toward the ground. Jerk it to wind it back up into your hand.

One-Handed Star

This is another simple picture trick. Start by letting the yo-yo hang. Then, take the string and lift it with your thumb. Then, wrap the string around your ring finger, then your index finger. Finally, wrap it around your middle finger and pinky finger. Once you have finished, wrap your thumb one more time to complete the picture. To dismount, you can easily let the yo-yo and the string drop off your fingers, before jerking upward so the yo-yo bounces back up into your hand.

Lariat

This trick is similar to Flying Saucer, because of the motion that the yo-yo makes at the end of the string. Instead of grabbing with your free hand, however, you will let the yo-yo go all the way to the end of the string as it moves down toward the ground. Use the finger of your free hand to start the yo-yo spinning, with the yo-yo lying down horizontally at the end of the string. Use a quick, strong tug to get the yo-yo to jump back up when you are ready for it to return to your hand.

Rattlesnake

Rattlesnake is very similar to the Lariat. The only difference is that when the yo-yo is at the end of the string, let the string touch the legs of your pants. It should make a rattling sound, which is what gives this trick its name.

The Creeper

This simple move is done on the floor. Start by throwing a Sleeper. Then, sway the yo-yo string back and forth until you can smoothly land it on the ground. Let the yo-yo roll out and away from you, before flicking your wrist to bring it back home. Note that your hand should be on the ground when you call the yo-yo back.

Front-style Bind

This trick is a simple return, but it is very effective when your yo-yo is not responsive. The key is the loop that is formed between the yo-yo and the string, with the finger of your free hand. Pull upward with the string while you use the index finger to line up the yo-yo so that the loop catches. As you feel the loop snag the yo-yo, let go and allow it to fall down into the loop. Then, jerk your hand so it returns home as it would in a simple Gravity Pull.

Spaghetti

Spaghetti is one of the simplest picture tricks. It mimics the motion of eating spaghetti. Start by throwing a hard sleeper. Then, bunch a few lengths of string and collect them in the fist of your yo-yo hand. Bring the hand up to your mouth and drop the yo-yo, making a slurping sound as the string falls. Then, make a show of wiping your mouth as the yo-yo bounces back up and into your hand.

The Jamaican Flag

For this picture trick, throw a hard sleeper. Then, use your free hand to pick up the hanging string so it is dangling from your empty hand. Use the hand holding the yo-yo to pull on the hanging part of the string, forming a triangle between your hands. Then, pick up the string with your empty hand and lift the string, pulling it across the middle part of the string to create an 'X' shape. Grip the string with your yo-yo hand and create the flagpole by letting the extra length of string hang down.

Chapter Two: Intermediate Yo-Yo Tricks

When you are ready to move past the stage of beginner, these are the best tricks to start improving your yo-yoing skills.

Split Bottom Mount

Start by throwing a Sleeper yo-yo. Then, use the pointer finger of your free hand to press against the string, about one-third of the way down. Use this to pull the string up as you lower the hand that is holding the yo-yo string. Next, use the finger of your yo-yo hand to press into the string as you flip the yo-yo forward, causing it to land on the front string (you should have a loop now). To complete the trick, bring your free hand down so that the yo-yo falls into the loop. This trick is similar to the Under Mount, but the yo-yo hangs on the loop because it is thrown over the yo-yo hand instead of over the free hand.

Orbit Launch
This trick is similar to Around the World, but it is a much shorter trip. Start by throwing a fast-spinning sleeper. Then, swing the yo-yo around your arm as you would during Around the World. Instead of allowing it to go full arc behind you, put your elbow out so it is parallel with your shoulder and allow it to drape over your arm. Then, use the hand of the same arm to pinch the string just above the yo-yo and jerk it upward so it jumps up and around your arm. Allow it to move down toward the floor before using a basic Gravity Pull to bring it back home.

Brain twister
You will start this trick by doing an Under Mount. Once the yo-yo is in position on the string, take your free hand and pull it up, so it is higher than your yo-yoing hand. Then, take the index finger of your hand that is holding the yo-yo string and pull back on the strings about halfway down. As you do this, swing the yo-yo so that it goes up and around your free hand. Do this a few times

before dismounting as you would from an Under Mount or by using a Ferris Wheel Dismount.

Stop and Go
To do this trick, throw a sleeper yo-yo. Then, use the left finger of your free hand and move it along the string, until you are two-thirds of the way down the string. Let the yo-yo swing back onto the string and hook there. Then, bring your hands together so that the free hand is positioned over the yo-yo hand. Your palms should be facing down.

To bring the yo-yo into the stop position, shake your hands so they move up. This should make the yo-yo swing into your open hands, creating the 'stop' position. Pull your yo-yo hand down and separate it from the left to make the yo-yo 'go.'

Eiffel Tower
To do the Eiffel Tower picture trick, start by throwing a Sleeper. Next, use your free hand to pull the yo-yo string up between your thumb and yo-yoing finger. You can shorten or lengthen the loop, depending on how big you'd like the tower to be. Next, use your free hand to twist the loop until the string hangs down. You should have a triangular shape, with the yo-yo hanging down on the string. Then, place either side of the base of the

tower on your yo-yo hand. Use your free hand to take hold of the string and use it to pull the upper part up, creating a 'Y' shape. Invert the 'Y' and you should have a picture of the Eiffel Tower.

Time Warp
This trick starts with Around the World, and then requires a backwards motion. Start by performing the Around the World trick. Once you have the yo-yo back in your hand, throw it backwards, in the opposite direction. It should move behind your back and swing around in front of your body. When you are ready to bring the yo-yo back to your hand, simply jerk it as you would during the typical Around the World trick. The same motion should bring it home.

The Bikini
Start by throwing a Sleeper yo-yo. Once the yo-yo is in position, grab the string with the fist of your free hand about one-third of the way down. Use the yo-yo hand to wrap the free part of the string around the string that you are holding tight with your fist. Then, use your yo-yo hand to grab onto the loop that is formed and pull it so you form a shape that looks like a pair of bikini bottoms. The yo-yo should dangle near the middle of the shape.

Next, you will create the bikini top. Swing the yo-yo so it loops up and around the two strings. When it loops around, it will pull them together, creating the shape of the bikini top. Open both fists and let the shape fall apart and then jerk upward to bring the yo-yo back home.

Wrist Mount
The Wrist Mount trick is useful to know because it serves as the base move for several other tricks. Begin as if you were doing a Double or Nothing, but instead of letting the yo-yo string wrap around the finger of your yo-yo hand, let it wrap around your wrist. Then, continue the yo-yo's motion so it goes around the point finger on your free hand and then land it on the string positioned in the middle. It should be the one that is coming from underneath the wrist.

Once in position, you can remove your free hand so that the yo-yo and string hang down. Turn your wrist sideways. The string that hangs down from the inside of your wrist and the yo-yo hand should create an 'X' shape, while the string on the outside of the wrist should stand alone. The yo-yo will be positioned at the bottom of this.

Robin Hood

For this picture trick, you let the yo-yo hang on the end of the string, pull it back as if you were an archer, and then release. Ideally, the yo-yo will be released and when it reaches the end of the length of string, it will bounce back up into your hand.

Begin with a Sleeper. Once in position, use the thumb of your yo-yo hand to create a 'C' shape. Then, use the index finger of your free hand to hook the yo-yo string and pull it back between the ends of that 'C' shape. Pull the string back until it is taut and then release. The yo-yo string will look like a mess, but if done correctly, it should straighten and the yo-yo should jump back into your hand.

Hop the Fence

This trick is a little harder than the Throw Down, but it makes great practice for learning the Loop the Loop trick from the next chapter. The major difference is that the yo-yo flips over when performing the Loop the Loop. To make this trick work, you need to change direction with each regeneration.

Start by performing a Throw Down. Instead of catching the yo-yo when it comes back toward your hand, move your yo-yo hand slightly so that the yo-yo goes up and around. Your palm should be facing upward, but do not catch the yo-yo. Instead, let it go up, around, and then fall down around your hand toward the ground. When it reaches the end of the string, jerk upward once again, this time moving your yo-yo hand forward so that it goes around the back of your hand and falls toward the front of it. Use the same slinging motion, but in the opposite direction. Continue doing this until you are satisfied and then bring the yo-yo back to your hand.

Houdini Mount

This yo-yo begins with the simple Breakaway trick. As the yo-yo swings around, stick out the thumb of your free hand about two-thirds of the way down the string. This and the trajectory will let the yo-yo continue moving up and around. As it comes around, move your hands closer together so that the yo-yo continues making a circle instead of mounting or coming to a stop. This should form a loop between your two hands, but the string should not be taut. This lets the yo-yo move freely.

As the yo-yo comes down, stick out the thumb of your yo-yo hand and let the string wrap around it. Do this again, keeping your hands close enough together that the yo-yo can continue to make loops. After it has wrapped around twice, mount the yo-yo on the string.

Trapeze

For this trick, you will start by doing a Breakaway. Once the yo-yo reaches the opposite side of your body, use the bottom of your pointer finger on your free hand to strike the yo-yo. As the string and your finger connect, the yo-yo should swing up and around. To complete the trick, the yo-yo should land on the 'wire' (yo-yo string) as a trapeze artist would. Mastering this is important for learning some more difficult moves. It is considered one of the easiest 'mounts', which are tricks where the yo-yo is 'mounted' on the string.

Double or Nothing

Double or Nothing is used in some other tricks, because it is easier to transition from than the Houdini Mount. It is incredibly similar, except as the yo-yo swings around after doing Breakaway, you will use your index finger on your free hand for the yo-yo to wrap around. Again, you will bring your hands closer together so that you can create two loops around your hands. Then, mount the yo-yo on the string. You can dismount from this using a Windmill Dismount, Flyaway Dismount or an Absolute Zero Dismount.

Triple or Nothing

To do this trick, start by performing a Double or Nothing, up until the point where you are ready to throw the yo-yo up and onto the string. Instead of landing the yo-yo on the string, throw it so it makes another round while you bring your hands closer. Then, throw the yo-yo up and let it land on the string farthest from your finger. Some yo-yos are even small enough that you can throw four or five loops (Quadruple or Nothing and Quintuple or Nothing). A Flyaway Dismount or Windmill Dismount are recommended for dismounting these tricks.

Windmill Dismount

This dismount is useful to know when you are dismounting after doing combos. If you have finished the Double or Nothing trick. Start the dismount by dropping the loops off the index finger of your yo-yo hand. With your free hand still holding the loops of string, you should have a single segment of string between your two hands and several loops of string hanging from your free hand.

Then, use the index finger of your empty hand to swing the yo-yo in a circle around your finger two or three times, until the extra loops have been unwound. This leaves you in perfect position to throw a Trapeze before dismount.

Ferris wheel Dismount

This is best performed after the yo-yo trick Under Mount, though it can be useful when your yo-yo is in a similar position in other tricks. With the yo-yo still on the string, pull upward with your yo-yo hand so the yo-yo is catapulted away from the string. The key to this trick is getting enough momentum, so do it quickly and with force. The yo-yo should follow its inertia around your free hand and out in front of you before moving upwards.

As it goes around, you will bring it back toward you by slightly tugging on the string. Allow it to swing around and make a full circle, going past your waists and then back up. As it continues forward, let it reach the end of its string before returning it to your hand as you would with a Forward Pass, but catch it from below. For a fancier dismount, add some Loop the Loop circles (discussed in the next chapter) before bringing it back into your hand.

One-and-a-Half Mount

This is similar to a Double or Nothing. Throw a Breakaway and then let the string go up and around, wrapping around your index finger on your free hand to create a loop. As the yo-yo circles around and drapes over the finger on your yo-yo hand, there should be just enough slack for the yo-yo to circle half-way around and land near the middle of the segment of string.

Waterfall

Waterfall is a picture trick, which you need to know Around the World for. Start by throwing the yo-yo as you would for the Around the World trick, but do it backwards. As the yo-yo moves up toward the sky and becomes level with your shoulder, swing the yo-yo so it wraps around your shoulder. Then, catch it near your elbow, making sure that the string stays on your arm and that there is a short length of string near the yo-yo end.

Take your free hand and reach it through the gap between the part of the string closest to you and the elbow. Then, pull the yo-yo out using the string and drop it so that it lands on the opposite side of the string closest to your body. This creates the image of water as it cascades over a cliff. When you are ready to dismount the yo-yo, straighten your arm at the elbow and let the string drop toward the ground. With practice, the goal is to throw the yo-yo up as the elbow string slides off, causing it to go into the air and wind itself.

Barrel Rolls

To do this trick, you will need to know how to do a Split Bottom Mount. Start by getting into position for the Split Bottom Mount. Then, use your free hand to move up and your yo-yo hand to move down, until they are level with each other and the yo-yo hangs on the loop approximately in the center of them. Next, take your free hand and pass it under the yo-yo before bringing it back up, this time positioning it behind the yo-yo hand. Then, take the yo-yo hand and perform the same movement as you flip the yo-yo up and over the yo-yo hand, until it is positioned back on the string to create the Split Bottom Mount again. Do this several times, until you are ready to dismount. Each time that you do this, the yo-yo string will become shorter as it winds around the index finger of your yo-yo hand.

Ripcord

Start with a Split Bottom Mount. Then, take the index finger of your free hand and insert it in the loop, grabbing the string that is closest to your body. Pull this string away from the other two. Then, swing the yo-yo so it lands on the two lengths of string closest to your body. Then, do this again and land the yo-yo on the string. Next, drop the string off the index finger of your yo-yo hand, stretching out the string. Then, drop the yo-yo and jerk it up as you would when doing a basic Gravity Pull.

Iron Whip
This is one of the earlier yo-yo tricks. For it to work, it is essential that you maintain even string tension. Begin with a Trapeze. Then, use the string to create an open loop. As you hold the loop open, pop the yo-yo so that it comes toward your body. Then, whip the loop so that it goes into the gap on the inside of the yo-yo. You should now be back in position for Trapeze. Catch the yo-yo to complete the trick.

Brother Mount
This trick is also called the Reverse Trapeze Mount. Start by doing a traditional Breakaway and moving into the Trapeze Mount. Once your yo-yo has landed on the string, take the middle finger of your free hand and extend it so you are pinching the string between your middle and forefinger. To dismount and complete the trick, tighten the string and sway the yo-yo so it goes up and over the hand that is not holding the yo-yo. As it travels under both hands, it will come around the back and do the Brother Mount, which is done properly when the yo-yo has been mounted on the string that is under your pointer finger. It should be the farthest away from your body. Dismount by pulling the string taut and allowing the yo-yo to travel up, around, and back down

and then move your free hand out of the way so the yo-yo can come back home.

Plastic Whip

This trick is best when done with an unresponsive yo-yo. Start by throwing a Sleeper. Then, take your yo-yo hand with the palm facing your opposite hand and make a 'U' shape. Now, you should have a string that runs down both over your thumb and your yo-yo finger. Next, create a loop with a jerk. Use the slack in the string to catch the yo-yo on the string.

Wave Slack

Use a Breakaway to throw a Trapeze. Then, use your empty hand to pinch the string and create slack under your yo-yo hand. Swing this slack around as you spin the yo-yo, alternating so you throw the slack and then the yo-yo. You do this by throwing and releasing the string that you pinched. When you are ready to finish the trick, throw the string so it lands back in Trapeze form and use it to catch the yo-yo.

Inner Rim Grind

While performing this trick, the goal is to 'grind' the inside part of the yo-yo on your thumb. This makes it essential that you have a decently sized inner edge between the two sides of the yo-yo, so part of your thumb can fit inside. Start by throwing a Trapeze, but do it so that the yo-yo is positioned near the edge of the trapeze, close to your thumb. Then, use your free hand to bring the trapeze together, sticking your thumb out so that the gap in the yo-yo lines up on your thumb. It is important that you hit the yo-yo without trapping the string. As you do this, the yo-yo should start to revolve.

Drop in the Bucket

Start by throwing a Sleeper. Then, put your free hand out with the palm facing upward. Push this against the string, so that it is hanging over the palm of your free hand. Next, use your yo-yo hand to wrap around the thumb and forefinger of your other hand, creating a curved length of string between the two. Then, take the index finger of your free hand and pull the loop of string off your thumb, pulling it toward your finger. You should have two outer parts that are the loop, as well as the length of the string that is holding the yo-yo. Then, swing the yo-yo up and over your hand, into the 'bucket' that you have created. The goal is to land the yo-yo on the string, as you would when doing a Trapeze.

Eli Hops

This trick is fairly simple if you can throw a Trapeze. Complete the Trapeze trick and then pull your hands apart, to make the yo-yo shoot upward. As it is moving up, bring your yo-yo hand and freehand closer again, creating a little lax in the string. Catch the yo-yo again and then send it flying. Continue doing this until you are ready to dismount.

Tsunami

This fun trick is popular among contestants in the world yo-yo contest, because it makes a nice picture and you can repeat as many times as you would like before dismounting or transitioning into another trick. Start by throwing a Breakaway that turns into a Sleeper. Once it is at the end of the string, swing it around and up so that the yo-yo goes into an Under Mount position. For this version of the trick, it is important that you use your index finger to create the Under Mount. Then, pop the yo-yo off the string and allow it to go back around, circling the index finger of your free hand. Repeat the trick by making the same movement to go into an Under Mount. When you are ready, catch the yo-yo.

Jade Whip

Start by going into a Trapeze. Then, bounce it back so that it hangs over the palm of your yo-yo hand. Pinch it, creating a loop with two of the outer fingers on your yo-yo hand. The string should go around and through the yo-yo. It may be easier to use your free hand to help you line up this yo-yo at first. The goal is to hop the yo-yo up once it is in position and then land it on the string. Then, you can let the pinch go so you are ready for dismount. To dismount, put your index finger of your free hand into the loop and swing the yo-yo so it rolls into the back string, going back into a Trapeze. Alternatively, you can roll onto the front string in front of the back like you are doing a Ripcord. Then, you can dismount using a bind.

Hourglass

To get in position for this trick, start by doing a One-and-a-Half Mount. Then, flip the yo-yo up and around to pop it around your other hand. Do not put the yo-yo through the triangle, but use the string to separate the rest into two separate triangles. The larger triangle should be on your empty hand, created with your thumb and pointer finger. It should look like a sideways hourglass with the yo-yo hanging down.

Then, you are going to try to land the yo-yo on the larger triangle by swinging it up and around. Pop it under the string and around, then make it land. Do this again but the opposite direction, going up and around before landing this time. Repeat the process as much as you would like. Be sure to swing it back through the triangle before dismounting to prevent a knot.

Sidewinder

This cool looking trick requires a responsive yo-yo. Start by throwing a Sleeper. Swing the string side to side, opposite the way the yo-yo is spinning. Make a swooping motion by swinging to one side and pulling to the other. For example, swinging to the right as you pull toward the left. This will get slack in the string that makes it wavy. The waves should catch on the yo-yo as the yo-yo is pulled up into the air, causing it to wind up in mid-air.

Chopsticks

This trick is also called Thumb Mount. Start by doing a Trapeze. Once in position, use the thumb of your free hand to press into the looped string between the free hand and the yo-yo. Then, bounce the yo-yo so it lands on the section between your thumb and pointer finger. When you are ready to dismount, release some of the string that is held by your yo-yo hand and make the yo-yo bounce out of the loop you have created. Swing the yo-yo so it goes into a Double or Nothing position and then use your choice of dismount.

Side-style Bind

If you can throw a Trapeze, this dismount should be easy to learn. You can throw the yo-yo into the air or transition from a pinwheel or other move. Stick out your finger to catch the string and let the yo-yo follow its path around it. As it catches the string, slacken it so the yo-yo can continue its trajectory down.

Wrist Whip

This trick is useful as you learn to move the string around for different tricks. It is similar to a Plastic Whip. Throw a Breakaway and let it hang straight down. Then, pull up with your yo-yo hand as you create a swooping motion to throw the yo-yo string over your wrist. Then, use your thumb and forefinger on that same hand to create a loop. This loop should whip into the yo-yo. The difficult part of this trick is to line up the yo-yo and string, especially since this trick is usually done with one hand.

Suicide

You will need to know how to throw a Trapeze to do this trick. Start by throwing a Breakaway and go into a Trapeze. Once in position, swing your free hand under your yo-yo hand and flick the finger of your free hand upwards, so you release the loop. The loop should now be traveling counter-clockwise around your yo-yo hand. Once the loop approaches the Trapeze position again, insert your finger to catch it.

Suicide One-and-a-Half

This is a modified version of the Suicide trick. The major difference is that you catch the loop that you create using your yo-yo hand. This puts you in a One-and-a-Half Mount. After you are in Trapeze, you will need to swing the yo-yo around so it comes across as you grab the string with your pointer finger to catch it and pull it away from the yo-yo.

Dizzy Baby

This move transitions from a Rock the Baby, so it is best to know this trick. Start by throwing the yo-yo into the Rock the Baby picture trick. To transition to Dizzy Baby, pinch the top of the string where the 'baby' is hanging from. Swing the yo-yo back and forth and then start to loop the yo-yo around the top of the string, going toward yourself then up and around. Do this as many times as you would like before dropping the yo-yo. It should not be tangled, but will fall toward the ground, ready for you to jerk it back up into your hand when it reaches the end of the string.

Chapter Three: Advanced Yo-Yo Tricks for the Experts

These advanced tricks are designed for people who have mastered the tricks listed in the previous chapter. They are one more step closer to joining the ranks of master yo-yo-ers around the world.

Flyaway Dismount

This trick is done following a Trapeze or Double or Nothing to dismount the yo-yo. Move your hands closer together so the yo-yo string has a little slack. Then, quickly pull your hands apart so the force bounces the yo-yo off the string and up toward the sky. Once the yo-yo has begun its motion, remove the finger of your free hand that was holding up the end of the 'trapeze.' Watch the yo-yo as it reaches the end of the rope, before jerking it so that it winds up. Catch it with your yo-yo hand.

Gyroscopic Flop
The yo-yo should rotate sideways on its access for this trick, while suspended in air. Start by throwing a Trapeze. Then, put your empty hand under the yo-yo so the string wraps around it. Then, use your yo-yo hand to pull the string taut and cause the yo-yo to spin. Keep the string horizontal and let the yo-yo gyrate. Binds are a great way to dismount this trick.

Loop the Loop
Begin by doing the Forward Pass trick, letting the yo-yo sleep for a second before swaying it so that it moves up and around. Then, tug it upward so that as it comes back, it makes a loop around your hand. You do not want to catch the yo-yo. Instead, bring your hand down so the yo-yo swings all the way around, before slinging it away from you again. It should perform the same motion, but it will be spinning in a different direction than before because the yo-yo will flip over during the transition. When you are satisfied with the number of loops that you have made, catch the yo-yo by letting it go

to the end of its string and jerking it back as you would when doing a Forward Pass.

Atom Smasher

To get in position for this trick, start by doing the Split Bottom Mount trick. Then, do an underpass with the yo-yo so that your hand that is holding the yo-yo is in front. Use your free hand and put it through the double string, switching the positions of your hands so the free hand is in front. Then, move the yo-yo hand down and under to do another underpass. Do several loops, or somersaults like you would while doing the Brain=twister trick. Dismount once you end the Brain-twister, either by pulling the string taut and releasing the yo-yo before calling it back home to your hand or by doing a Ferris Wheel Dismount.

Hidemasa Hook

This trick will be easiest if you are familiar with the Reverse Slack Trapeze. Start by throwing the Breakaway move, but let the yo-yo dangle at the end. As you pull upward, whip the string so you form a loop that goes down, as the yo-yo moves upward. The loop should fall under the pointer finger of your free hand. The yo-yo should be hovering by the same finger at this point. The string should continue moving around the finger until it catches in the gap of the yo-yo.

Next, pull the string taut. You should have the yo-yo on a loop, similar to the way it would be when doing a Reverse Trapeze. Then, use a Windmill Dismount (or something else) to impress as you call the yo-yo back home. This will leave you in a Trapeze and if you choose, you can use a Side-style Back Bind.

Pop the Clutch
For this trick, you will start with a Sleeper yo-yo. Take the elbow of your free hand and tuck it in as you pull the yo-yo string up and swing it toward the back of your body. This should wrap it around your elbow and shoulder, forming an upside down 'U' shape that goes over your shoulder. Then, you are going to use your thumb and forefinger on your free hand to pull the yo-yo and pop it back up and over your shoulder. It should land back in your hand. If you cannot get it, you may need to adjust the power behind your throw or use more or less fore when you pull the yo-yo to send it back up.

Mach 5
The Mach 5 is an illusionary trick, which makes it seem as if the yo-yo is floating in mid-air as your hands move around it. The key to mastery is getting the yo-yo to hold

its same position as you move your hands. Begin by throwing a Split Bottom Mount. Instead of the yo-yo being positioned toward the bottom of the string when you mount it, however, you want it to be positioned evenly between your hands.

Pull the hand opposite your yo-yo hand down and away from your body, letting the yo-yo suspend itself on the string between your hands. Then, rotate both your hands, being sure to keep the same pace for each of them. Do this as many times as you would like, being sure to keep the string tight so the yo-yo cannot move. To end the trick, put your hands in position so the yo-yo hand is the one closest to you. Pull the yo-yo hand finger out of the loop and dismount the yo-yo.

Magic Drop
This trick can be frustrating, because you do not want all the strings to land in the gap of the yo-yo. Start by throwing a Trapeze. Then, take the thumb on your yo-yo hand and point it toward the finger. Twist the string in toward yourself and stretch it between your thumb and pointer finger. This should create a triangle between your thumb, index, and middle finger.

Next, swing the yo-yo until it has enough inertia to go up and around your hand. It should swing over and up onto the string stretching between your two hands. It will fall up and over the pointer finger before falling into place.

Absolute Zero
This cool trick starts in position for Double or Nothing. Alternatively, you can start this position with the Absolute Zero Dismount. Once in position, pop the yo-yo off the string and let it fall onto the one farthest from your body. Then, throw the yo-yo up again as you drop the string that is farthest from your body. When the yo-yo lands, you should be in Trapeze position. Then, move your yo-yo hand down the string as you pop the yo-yo again, landing in position for Brother Mount. As you jump the yo-yo into the air again, you will get it in position for Double or Nothing.

Finally, pull the finger of your yo-yo string out of the loop around it. Swing the yo-yo so it moves toward your free hand. Throw the yo-yo down using the hand that is holding it and jerk upward on the string to bounce it back into your hand.

Absolute Zero Dismount
This trick is best for an unresponsive yo-yo. Start in position for the end of the trick Double or Nothing. Then, toss the yo-yo into the air as you drop the first loop that is around the index finger of your empty hand.

Then, throw the yo-yo up and pull your hands apart to tighten the string. Try to land the yo-yo on the stretch of string that is farthest from your body. Next, drop the loop that is around the finger of your yo-yo hand, pull your hands apart, and land in a basic Trapeze.

Pop-N-Fresh

To master this trick, you will need to begin in the Split Bottom Mount and be able to move into the Mach 5 trick. After positioning for the end of the Split Bottom Mount, pull the string tight so the yo-yo 'pops' into the air. While it is up, switch the places of your hands, passing your free hand over your hand that holds the yo-yo. Once you do this, the end result with the yo-yo lands should be a Mach 5 mount. Pop the yo-yo again when in position, reversing them so that the yo-yo hand passes over the free hand. This should leave you in a Split Bottom Mount. You can do this as many times as you would like before dismounting.

Wormhole

Knowing the Ripcord is useful when doing this trick. Start with the Split Bottom Mount and then go into Ripcord. Next, put your pointer finger back into the string and bring it around. Use the pointer finger of your yo-yo hand and pass under the free hand. Next, do the

Ripcord but swing the yo-yo away from your body instead of toward it. Loop this twice, then drop the pointer finger and pull back. Dismount as you would when doing Brain-twister.

Lindy Loop

The Lindy Loop is an advanced version of the Trapeze yo-yo trick. Start by doing a Trapeze, swinging the yo-yo up and around the finger of your free hand so that the yo-yo lands on the string. Once it is in position, flip both your hands so that the yo-yo is on the side. Naturally, it should start to swing in a downward motion.

Sway the yo-yo string so that it goes up and around the pointer finger of your free hand again. Your goal is to re-mount the yo-yo on the string. After you have completed the trick, flip the yo-yo again, this time letting it fall to the ground and then jerk upward to bring it back to your hand.

Ghost Rider

Start by throwing a Sleeper. Once in position, let the yo-yo stay there as you gently take the loop off your throwing finger, pinching it between your pointer finger and thumb. Then, yank the string up so that the yo-yo starts to move toward you. Then, release the string. As the yo-yo comes back down, you will catch it.

Mondial

Start with a Split Bottom Mount and move into the beginning of the Mach 5 trick, moving your hands forward to get the yo-yo on the string. Then, pop the string by pulling it taut. As the yo-yo goes up, you will separate the strings by crossing your hands. Then, land the yo-yo on the string that is coming from your yo-yoing finger. This will leave you in a Split Bottom Mount.

Kwijibo

This advanced trick takes some practice, but it is well worth it. Start by throwing a Trapeze. Next, pop the yo-yo up and throw it over the index finger of your throwing hand. As you do this, cross your hands so the yo-yo lands on the string. Your throw hand will go into the strings, while the free hand will just come across. Then, swing the yo-yo toward your yo-yo hand, keeping it on the sting. Uncross your hands as you swing the yo-yo over. Then, re-cross them in the opposite direction to toss the yo-yo back and forth.

Next, toss the yo-yo as you pull on the strings and bring your index finger of your yo-yo hand into the strings. This should leave you in position for a Double or Nothing. Dismount how you choose to.

Buddha's Revenge

Throw the yo-yo so it wraps around the index finger of your opposite hand before coming back around and wrapping around your yo-yo hand index finger into a One-and-a-Half Mount. Then, hold onto the loop as you take the finger of your free hand and swing the yo-yo over your hands. The yo-yo should stay on the string as you do this. Next, swing back into a One-and-a-Half Mount. Then, dismount into a Trapeze.

McBride Roller Coaster

This trick is actually a series of tricks, making it a great combo when you want to show off your flair. Start by throwing the yo-yo up and around, using a combination of Breakaway and Around the World to go into One-and-a-Half Mount. Then, swing the yo-yo in the opposite direction into Trapeze and His Brother. Once in position, you will be throwing again, rolling the yo-yo into a Triple or Nothing. Drop all the strings after the Triple or Nothing, dismounting it as you choose.

Cold Fusion

Start by throwing a Double or Nothing. Bring your free hand down and use it to catch the yo-yo on the outside string. Then, pull your finger out, leaving the string so you are in a One-and-a-Half Mount. Then, swing the yo-yo over your free hand, before passing it back over and hanging it once again into a One-and-a-Half Mount. To dismount, unwrap the loop twice by swinging the yo-yo around and pull it back into a Trapeze, neatly catching the yo-yo between your hands.

Split the Atom

You will need to have practice with several tricks to perform Split the Atom, including Split Bottom Mount, Double or nothing, and Under Mount. Begin with the Split Bottom Mount. Then, take your free hand and do a forward underpass, bringing your hand around and under the yo-yo before returning to its original position. Then, do an underpass in the opposite direction, ensuring that the yo-yo ends up on the part of the string that does not form the loop. This is position for Double or Nothing.

Once in position, make three loops with the yo-yo, which are also called somersaults. Drop the second string that creates the loop by removing it from the pointer finger of your yo-yo hand. The position at the end of this should be the same as the one for Under Mount. Then, you can use a simple dismount or finish with a Ferris Wheel Dismount.

Slack Trapeze

Being familiar with the Trapeze will help when completing this trick. This is a slack trick, which is a trick completed with the yo-yo when the string is slack and the yo-yo is motionless. Start by pinching the end of the string near the yo-yo with your empty and. Then, swing the yo-yo string segment you have created upward. As it goes up, swing it so that it jumps over the wrist of your empty hand. As you do this, whip the yo-yo string down so part of it lands in the yo-yo. Once the string is securely in the yo-yo, separate your hands to pull the string taut. Next, use the length of string to swing the yo-yo over and around your empty hand, doing a pinwheel and to throw the yo-yo into Trapeze position.

Reverse Slack Trapeze

If you want to throw a combo, consider ending it with this impressive trick. To get in position to do this trick, start by throwing a Trapeze. Next, pinch the loop of string with the hand that is not holding the yo-yo and use it to throw the string toward the ground. As you do this, sling the loop so it goes under and around your free hand wrist. As you do this, direct the yo-yo toward the string so one of the strands catches in the inner gap of the yo-yo. Next, pull the string taut and do a Windmill

Dismount. After completing this, you can throw a Side-style Bind.

Dr. Strange

For this trick, you will start in a Double or Nothing. Then, cross your hands by taking the index finger of your yo-yo hand (and the string) up and over your empty hand. Pull it tight and bring the hands around each other in a circular motion, similar to what you would do for a Mach 5. Then, drop the string attached to the yo-yo hand into a gap, bringing your hands together and then swinging the yo-yo around twice to unwrap the twisting. Be careful not to follow the yo-yo with your hands, otherwise they will not untwist. This will leave you in a Trapeze, which you can easily dismount how you choose to.

Trapeze Triangle Slack

When done properly, this trick is very smooth. Knowing how to do a Wrist Mount will be helpful when doing this trick. Start by doing a Trapeze. Then, throw the string as you would when doing a Wrist Mount, looping it around your throw hand. As the string goes under the yo-yo, drop it. The yo-yo should end up on the string, while the position on your wrist and your index finger should create a triangular shape. Note that there will still be a length of string running from the yo-yo to your free hand, which is not part of the triangle shape.

Black Hops

You will need to be able to do a Triple or Nothing to do this trick. Start by throwing a Triple or Nothing. Then, pop the yo-yo up and around as you pull your hands apart slightly, so that when it lands you are in position for a Double or Nothing. From here, you are going to pop the yo-yo up again and land it into a Trapeze. Then, do the trick in reverse by going from the Trapeze to a Double or Nothing and then into a Triple or Nothing. You can do this trick as many times as you would like before deciding how to dismount.

Boomerang

This is similar to the Boingy-Boing trick, especially because of the importance of timing to get the trick right. Start by throwing a Brain twister, by draping the string over the index finger of your free hand. Then, rock the yo-yo back and forth over your finger, pulling your finger up and down to make the yo-yo swing. Once you can line up the timing and land the string, try pulling down on the string with your yo-yo hand. Your goal is to throw the yo-yo on and off the string, eventually being able to let the yo-yo reach the end of the string before bringing it back to connect with the string.

Shockwave

Knowing Magic Drop is essential for this trick, which can be performed repeatedly until you get tired of it. Start with a Trapeze and then land a Magic Drop. Then, take the index finger of your yo-yo hand and curve it around, so it is pointing in toward yourself. Then, take the index finger on your free hand and push it between the two strings coming from the index finger of your yo-yo hand. Next, swing the yo-yo up and around and land it on the string that is closest to your body. Pull the index finger of your yo-yo hand out to drop off the strings and you can easily get back into Trapeze, ready to perform the trick again.

The Matrix

This is a great combination trick. Start by throwing a Double or Nothing. Then, drop the pointer finger of your yo-yo hand and roll the yo-yo off your finger, going into a Trapeze. Then, you will roll the yo-yo by throwing it over your finger on your yo-yo hand and going back into a Double or Nothing.

To make the trick look smooth, you do an extra roll by taking the finger of your yo-yo hand and moving it up and around the finger of your free hand. Do this as you transition from the Double or Nothing into a Trapeze.

Boingy Boing

This is a complicated trick that will take a lot of practice. Start in a Split Bottom Mount, allowing the yo-yo string to form a loop around your index finger of your yo-yo hand and holding your free hand above it. You want to position the yo-yo so it is about halfway between each of your hands. Once in position, pull up with the index finger of your free hand to cause the yo-yo to bounce forward. The goal is to get the yo-yo to bounce between each of the strings by jerking the index finger of your hand up and down to create and reduce tension in the string.

Once you have the basic movement down, it is time to practice the trick. Bounce the yo-yo back and forth between the two strings very quickly. When you are ready to dismount, do so as you would when performing the Split Bottom Mount trick.

Over Under Boingy Boing

You will need to know how to do Boingy Boing for this trick. Essentially, you can switch the two tricks back and forth for a really cool display. Start with a Split Bottom Mount and do the Boingy Boing. Then, start to swing the yo-yo under the index finger of your bottom hand, allowing it to swing under and then come back around into the Boingy Booing motion. Once you are comfortable going toward your body, start to move forward, down, and around. As you practice, you will find yourself ready to move faster and switch between the tricks. This will make the trick smoother.

Spirit Bomb

This trick can be a little tricky to get the hang of, especially since the entire time it looks like you may get the yo-yo string tangled up into a knot. Start by doing a Wrist Mount and allowing the yo-yo to hang free after it is in position, with the single string on one side and the 'X' shape on the other. Then, use the index finger of your free hand to push against the string that is against your wrist (on the outside). Push the string down and around the yo-yo, causing the yo-yo to jump over and land on the string. This will form three triangle-like shapes with the string. Essentially, the yo-yo is popping up through the 'X' shape and then landing on the standalone string. You will cross the two hands over each other as you perform the trick.

Next, swing the yo-yo back to where you started. Then, pop the yo-yo out through the string, so it is swinging freely.

The Zipper
This trick requires a repetition of vertical movements, which are easier if you know how to mount for a Brain-twister. Basically, you will be throwing the yo-yo and then having it swing up and around, pushing into the strings as it would when you mount for Brain-twister. Stick your thumb out once you are ready to re-mount, using it to get the yo-yo on the string. Throwback onto the thumb, re-thread they yo-yo into a Brain-twister Mount, and then go up and over, using the thumb of your free hand once again. The key to this trick is smoothness, which will come as you become faster and more fluid while performing the trick.

Laceration
There are several variations of this trick, because the true trick is incredibly difficult. This will be the simplest interpretation and the more complex version will be included next. Start by throwing a Breakaway and then let it hang. Then, use the motion of a wrist whip to create a loop. Once you can create a loop, catch it using your free hand index finger. In the same motion, you should be able to land the laceration on a string. The true Laceration move starts in a Trapeze. Then, you follow the same steps to get into the Laceration. The key is timing and being able to line up the whip of the string

with the yo-yo, so you can land it as you pull the string tight.

Leg Wrap Trapeze

This is a very showy trick, making it great for a performance. Start with a Breakaway, then put one of your legs out in front of the other and swing the yo-yo around it. You should have a revolution around your leg as you move your other leg forward. Then, grab the yo-yo and swing through the legs again. As you go behind the second leg, put out the finger of your free hand and use it to move into a Trapeze.

Superman

Knowing how to do Spirit Bomb is essential to this trick. Start as you would when mounting for Spirit Bomb. This should create a triangle on your yo-yo hand. To do Superman, throw the yo-yo so it goes through the triangle that you have created by grabbing the string with your index finger of your free hand. Throw it through the triangle closest to your body.

Then, pop the yo-yo back up and land it on two strings, as if you were doing a Spirit Bomb. Then, swing the yo-yo around and over your hand, causing it to come off the strings and then landing it on the string farthest from your body.

Kamikaze

This is a lengthy trick, but it is a series of some stuff that you may have already learned. Knowing Magic Drop is essential for this trick. Start by throwing the Houdini Mount, catching the yo-yo with your thumb and index fingers. Then, pop the yo-yo so it moves up into the loop that you are holding with your thumb. Move your thumb out and then swing the yo-yo around, causing it to land on the string closest to your body.

Next, take the index finger of your free hand to pull in on the string. Pop the yo-yo up so that it lands on the top string. Then, drop the index finger on your free hand as you swing the yo-yo around your hand. This will stop it from falling. This puts it into a Trapeze. Then, you do a Magic Drop. After doing this, you flip the yo-yo up and around and catch it on the string.

Skin the Gerbil

This is a fun trick, because it looks like the yo-yo is bouncing all around on the strings. Start with a Trapeze. Then, take your yo-yo hand and turn it inward before using it to push on the string, causing it to go up and around. Then, land on two of the strings as the yo-yo lands.

Swing the yo-yo around your hand the opposite way next, before swinging it around so it goes around your yo-yo hand and lands on the strings. Then, loop the string around your finger as you did in the Matrix move, so you can dismount without getting any knots in your string.

Conclusion

Thank you for downloading this book! Now that you have reached the end of it, you should find yourself more than ready to excel at some of the beginner moves. As you advance through these, you will find that the intermediate and advanced tricks start to seem a bit easier.

There are many great resources online that can help, especially now that you have the basic knowledge of how each trick is done. Look up picture instructions or video tutorials if anything seems confusing. Once it becomes clear, you will find yourself ready to yo-yo with the pros in no time.

Enjoy and good luck!

Hey,

I sincerely hope that you feel inspired by the 101 Yo-Yo Tricks and could learn a ton of new tricks to impress your friends!

Before you close this book I´d like to ask you could do me a favor and leave an honest review on amazon. On Amazon reviews are the bread and butter for every author and without them our books will not get bought. So, you would to me a great favor if you spend a minute to leave me a review.

THANK YOU!

References

https://www.thoughtco.com/the-history-of-the-yo-yo-1992695

https://entertainment.howstuffworks.com/easy-yo-yo-tricks.htm

http://yoyoempire.com/index.php?option=com_content&view=article&id=10&itemid=9

http://www.classicyoyotricks.com/yoyo-trick-list/

https://www.hasbro.com/common/instruct/YoYo_FAST_Quick_Start_and_Trick_Chart_Guide.pdf

https://yoyotricks.com/

https://yoyoexpert.com/learn-2-point-0/

CPSIA information can be obtained
at www.ICGtesting.com
Printed in the USA
BVHW041841081221
623566BV00014B/1032

9 783907 269077